CONTENTS

INTRODUCTION

SCHOOL CAN BE FUN AT TIMES, but you're mainly there to learn things. Crosswords are sort of the opposite: you'll learn things at times, but you're mainly there to have fun.

The puzzles in this book are filled with things you probably know a lot about—food, animals, movies, games, and so on—but once in a while there might be something you don't know. So that's one of those times when you'll learn something; if you can't figure it out from the crossing words, just ask someone else. That's not cheating!

I hope you have a lot of fun!

—*Trip Payne*

ACROSS

1 What a red light means to a driver
5 Flower that hasn't opened yet
8 Face ___ (type of plastic surgery)
12 Beatles singer ___ McCartney
13 Find a purpose for
14 Notion
15 Directions in this puzzle: 3 words
18 Opposite of dry
19 Words of rejection
20 Copper fastener on Levi's jeans
23 Large
24 Pet that purrs
27 Liquid inside a battery
28 Many kids ride to school on one
29 Destiny
30 Where a bodybuilder might work out
31 "How stupid do you think ___?": 2 words
32 Tokyo's country
33 "Raggedy" doll
34 Devour
35 Colors in this puzzle: 3 words

42 Incorrect way to say "isn't" or "aren't"
43 Broken-down horse
44 Wicked
45 Tools for catching butterflies or fish
46 Gorilla, for example
47 Smell really bad

DOWN

1 Health resort
2 Tic-___-toe
3 "It'll be ___ little secret"
4 Cleared snow from the streets
5 Go over 21, in blackjack
6 Country between Canada and Mexico: Abbreviation
7 "___ the Menace" (comic strip)
8 Jar tops
9 Wedding ceremony vow: 2 words
10 ___ and far between
11 Light brown color
16 "Ready, ___, go!"
17 Hound
20 Old, dirty cloth
21 Frosty

22 ___ and vigor (enthusiasm)

23 Hobo

24 What a baseball player wears on the head

25 Take things one step ___ time: 2 words

26 Five times two

28 Yellow fruit

29 Dad

31 Liquid used in tattoos

32 Mouth bone

33 Performs in a movie

34 Outer border

35 Ray-___ (brand of sunglasses)

36 Say something dishonest

37 Hard-working insect

38 Daytime snooze

39 "___ changed my mind"

40 Score where neither side is ahead

41 Large animal in the deer family

2

ACROSS

1 Small plastic thing you might find on a necklace
5 Half of four
8 Frying ___ (kitchen tool)
11 Item from the distant past that someone might dig up
13 Meat that comes from a pig
14 "You ___ me an explanation"
15 What Muslims call God
16 Organ of sight
17 Use a needle and thread
18 "Mona ___" (famous painting)
20 "Ready or ___, here I come!"
22 School fund-raising group: Abbreviation
25 Hot stuff that comes out of a volcano
27 Autumn
30 Superhero group that includes Superman and Wonder Woman: 2 words
33 Surprise in a big way
34 Fort ___ (where American gold is stored)
35 Food that might be fried or scrambled
36 Pigpen
38 Receives
40 "What do ___ want?"
42 Female sheep
44 Wall-E, for one

48 Apple pie ___ mode: 2 words
49 Black material used for paving roads
50 All by yourself
51 Sideshow ___ (Krusty's sidekick after Sideshow Bob, on "The Simpsons")
52 Cards that prove who you are: Abbreviation
53 Large farm animals that sometimes pull plows

DOWN

1 What a woman might wear underneath a blouse
2 Electric ___ (fish that could shock you)
3 Everything
4 What you turn on a car radio
5 Superhero group that includes Iron Man and Thor: 2 words
6 Milky ___ (candy bar)
7 Bad sign of what's coming in the future
8 How much it costs to mail something
9 ___-inspiring (really impressive)
10 Opposite of old
12 Food that often contains meat and beans

Crossword Grid

Grid cells numbered: 1 2 3 4 — 5 6 7 — 8 9 10 / 11 12 13 14 / 15 16 17 / 18 19 20 21 / 22 23 24 25 26 27 28 29 / 30 31 32 / 33 34 35 / 36 37 38 39 / 40 41 42 43 44 45 46 47 / 48 49 50 / 51 52 53

19 Burlap bag

21 "Diary ___ Wimpy Kid": 2 words

22 Clothes you wear to bed, for short

23 King ___ (ancient Egyptian ruler who has a famous tomb)

24 Like you normally do: 2 words

26 ___ vera (soothing ingredient found in some hand creams)

28 Carry around

29 Chicken drumstick

31 Explosive stuff: Abbreviation

32 Go the ___ mile (do more than you have to)

37 Mythical creature that's also known as the Abominable Snowman

39 Han ___ (character in "Star Wars")

40 Another name for a sweet potato

41 What people yell at a bullfight

43 Glob of chewing gum

45 Container that's often made from cardboard

46 Go back to square ___ (start over)

47 King's value in blackjack

ACROSS

1 Tool that has sharp teeth
4 Optimist's feeling
8 Practice for a boxing match
12 "Three, two, ___, blastoff!"
13 Location
14 First name of the wife of England's Prince William
15 Pro football team from Pittsburgh
17 Frosted, like a birthday cake
18 ___-hoo (chocolate-flavored drink)
19 Chore
21 "You can't ___ your cake and eat it too"
24 Plead
25 ___ and flow (movements of the tide)
28 "___ Baba and the Forty Thieves"
29 In that place
31 Kanga's kid in "Winnie-the-Pooh"
32 Big, shaggy animal from Asia
33 ___ up (crumple)
34 Game where you try to observe things: 2 words
35 ___-on patch
37 Fuel for a car
39 ___, Pinta, and Santa María (Columbus's ships)
41 Pro football team from Seattle
46 Like humor that pushes boundaries
47 Brand of frozen waffles
48 Cool and modern
49 Throw gently
50 ___ and found department
51 "Based ___ true story": 2 words

DOWN

1 Letters that mean "Emergency!"
2 Bug that might be a snack for an aardvark
3 "___ Willie Winkie"
4 Circle over an angel's head
5 Black-and-white cookie
6 Miles ___ hour (what "MPH" means to a driver)
7 Holiday when many people dye eggs
8 Goes down a snowy hill
9 Pro football team from Green Bay
10 Devoured
11 Main color of a stop sign
16 It winks and blinks

20 "When I was your ___ ..."
21 Grass that's put into bales on a farm
22 State whose capital is Montgomery: Abbreviation
23 Pro football team from Minnesota
24 Place to sleep
26 "Kidz ___" (series of albums for kids)
27 Young man
29 Lowest number you can roll with a pair of dice
30 Gretel's brother

34 "This ___ stickup!": 2 words
36 Beams of sunlight
37 Practical jokes
38 On ___ streak (winning big): 2 words
39 Safety device underneath a trapeze
40 Pledge from a bride and groom: 2 words
42 Anton ___ (restaurant critic in "Ratatouille")
43 "Horton Hears a ___!" (Dr. Seuss book)
44 Family members
45 Health resort

4

ACROSS

1 Police officers
5 "___ sells seashells by the seashore" (tongue twister)
8 A witch might wear a pointy one
11 Mystical glow that a psychic might claim to "read"
12 Capture, as a criminal
13 ___-Wan Kenobi ("Star Wars" character)
14 Large, extinct animal whose name comes from the Greek for "thunder lizard"
17 The Dynamic ___ (nickname for Batman and Robin)
18 12-month periods: Abbreviation
19 Sleeping ___ (item for a camper)
22 Device that tells a driver where to go: Abbreviation
24 Sour, yellow fruit
28 Person from the Middle East, often
30 "You bet!"
32 Not crazy
33 Facing a baseball pitcher: 2 words
35 Something you download to a phone or tablet

37 Water droplets on blades of grass
38 ___ Angeles, California
40 "___ been a pleasure"
42 Extinct birdlike animal that was featured in "Jurassic Park"
48 How a sailor would say 30-Across
49 Pretty ___ picture: 2 words
50 State whose capital is Des Moines
51 It's in the middle of a tennis court
52 Sports league that involves pucks and skates: Abbreviation
53 "Big top" at a circus

DOWN

1 Taxi
2 "Be ___ Guest" (song in "Beauty and the Beast")
3 Expert
4 What castles on the beach are made of
5 Charlie Brown's dog
6 "This ___ nothing to do with you"
7 Website that runs online auctions
8 "Hold your ___!" ("Just wait a minute!")

9 Monkey friend of Aladdin

10 "My country, ___ of thee ..."

15 ___-of-war (game that uses a rope)

16 Internet address: Abbreviation

19 Lamb's cry

20 Paintings and sculptures

21 Talk a lot

23 Large body of water

25 Furious

26 Half of two

27 Not old

29 "Swan Lake," for example

31 ___ staircase (curvy thing to climb)

34 "It's never ___ late"

36 Elementary school support group: Abbreviation

39 Quickly read over

41 What a dentist might tell you to do when you have a mouth full of water

42 Movers' vehicle

43 Hole in a needle

44 Ending for "fool" or "fiend"

45 Body part with a nail

46 Possess

47 Rodent that eats cheese

5

ACROSS

1 ___ the Builder (animated character who constructs things)
4 Drink that can be served hot or cold
7 Like a dog that can transmit disease
12 "Not ___ million years!": 2 words
13 Paddle that moves a boat
14 Opposite of below
15 "Beat it!": 2 words
17 Shakespeare wrote them
18 Small clue
19 Boat's docking place
20 Destroys
22 Terrible
23 Apply gently, like makeup
26 "That ___ fair!"
27 Purchase
28 Small bit of land that's surrounded by water
29 "I ___ your pardon?"
30 What three strikes make, in baseball
31 Felt sore
32 Drinks through a straw
34 Nabisco cookie
35 Make happen
37 ___ Mountains (sweet area in the game Candy Land)
40 Creature from another planet
41 Card that's worth 1 or 11 in blackjack
42 Prefix that means "three"
43 Nibbles
44 Advanced degree from a university: Abbreviation
45 "Let me ___ the record straight ..."

DOWN

1 Massive
2 "___ thing leads to another"
3 Something you might wear to the beach: 2 words
4 Bugs Bunny and Popeye, for example
5 Direction of the rising sun
6 What museums display
7 Quick
8 Ready, willing, and ___
9 Something you might wear to the beach: 2 words
10 Plant that can climb a wall

11 ___ Moines (Iowa's capital)

16 Fuzz you might find in a pocket of your pants

19 ___ attention (listen closely)

20 Bone in the chest

21 Put into operation

22 "Thanks, ___ no thanks"

24 Ginger ___ (bubbly beverage)

25 Piece of furniture in a hotel room

27 ___ driver (Otto's job on "The Simpsons")

28 Covered with frosting

30 Unwraps

31 ___ and dangerous (like some criminals)

33 "Peekaboo, ___ you!": 2 words

34 "That hurts!"

35 Taxi

36 Boxer Muhammad ___

37 Empty space between two teeth

38 Rock sought by miners

39 ___ bull terrier (kind of dog)

6

ACROSS

1 Paddington, for one
5 Ending for "lemon" or "lime"
8 Performs in a play
12 Frozen breakfast brand that makes French Toaster Sticks
13 Disney dwarf with the shortest name
14 State that borders South Dakota and Nebraska
15 Kids' book about going to sleep: 2 words
18 Feeling gloomy
19 French word for "yes"
20 Golfer's target score
23 What to fill a car's tank with
25 Annoying little bugs
29 State where Cincinnati is
31 Used a chair
33 ___ club (high school singing group)
34 ___ Bay Buccaneers (NFL team)
36 Really ticked off
38 Allow
39 Supposed psychic power: Abbreviation
41 Daughter's brother
43 Kids' book about a girl and her notebook: 3 words

50 Location
51 Body part involved in kicking
52 Cord that electricity travels through
53 Marries
54 Piece of turf
55 "X marks the ___"

DOWN

1 Ask for spare change
2 Vain person's problem
3 "A long time ___ in a galaxy far, far away ..."
4 Fishing poles
5 Competitor of Reebok and Nike
6 Hound
7 Sound effect heard in a cave
8 Lining up an arrow with the target, in archery
9 Sound made by a pigeon
10 Half of four
11 ___ Francisco, California
16 Constantly remind
17 ___-of-war (game using a rope)
20 Vessel to make spaghetti in

A crossword grid numbered with cells: 1-11 across top, then 12, 13, 14; 15, 16, 17; 18, 19; 20, 21, 22, 23, 24, 25, 26, 27, 28; 29, 30, 31, 32, 33; 34, 35, 36, 37, 38; 39, 40, 41, 42; 43, 44, 45, 46, 47, 48, 49; 50, 51, 52; 53, 54, 55.

21 "Now I get it!"

22 Outer edge of a basketball hoop

24 Uncle ___ (symbol of America)

26 "... with liberty and justice for ___"

27 Type of casual, short-sleeved shirt

28 "Quiet on the ___!" (director's cry)

30 Music performances where sopranos might sing in Italian

32 Sampled, like soup

35 "Just ___ suspected!": 2 words

37 Play-___ (brand of modeling clay)

40 Household dogs and cats

42 What's happening in the world

43 Hee-___ (donkey's sound)

44 "How old ___ you?"

45 Color of a cherry

46 "___ much information!"

47 Slowly enjoy a drink

48 Big-league athlete

49 Up to now

ACROSS

1 Soft drinks
6 Tiny ___ (character in "A Christmas Carol")
9 Profession
12 Where a pro basketball team plays
13 Wedding vow: 2 words
14 Female sheep
15 Marge and Selma's sister, on "The Simpsons"
16 The largest city in Washington, but not its capital
18 Three-___ circus
20 "This is ___-brainer!": 2 words
21 Male version of "sis"
23 Tree that drops acorns
25 What's left after something burns
29 Surprise attack by the police
31 Polite way to address a man
33 Just average: Hyphenated
34 Room at the top of a house
36 ___-tac-toe
38 ___ and downs
39 Get a look at
41 Physicians, for short
43 The largest city in Illinois, but not its capital

47 "Live free or die," for New Hampshire
50 Close friend of Harry and Hermione, in the Harry Potter books
51 Father's boy
52 Hello or goodbye, in Hawaii
53 Money used in Tokyo
54 Ending for "Vietnam" or "Japan"
55 Less crazy

DOWN

1 Sticky stuff on a pine tree
2 "Would you like a cup ___ cone?" (question at an ice cream shop): 2 words
3 The largest city in Michigan, but not its capital
4 Prefix meaning "against"
5 "Just ___ to drugs": 2 words
6 "___ the season to be jolly …"
7 Creative thought
8 Disney movie that features a dumb rooster named Heihei
9 Fast plane

10 Bird that hoots
11 Honey maker
17 Throw, like a horseshoe
19 Fuel for an automobile
21 What a woman wears under a blouse
22 Pack ___ (person who saves everything)
24 First-aid ___
26 The largest city in Texas, but not its capital
27 Psychic's "sixth sense": Abbreviation
28 Sailors' distress signal
30 Compact ___ player
32 Got ___ of (threw away)

35 Halt
37 Long-lasting periods of unconsciousness
40 Vain people have big ones
42 Coke or Pepsi, for example
43 Weep
44 Garden tool with a flat blade
45 Holiday ___ (hotel chain)
46 ___ Direction (British boy band)
48 Most common word in English
49 Paddle for a canoe

ACROSS

1 "It's the moment everyone ___ been waiting for!"
4 Major network that isn't ABC, NBC, or Fox: Abbreviation
7 Mix with a spoon
11 Aladdin's pet monkey in the Disney movie
12 Started, like a fire
13 What elephant tusks are made of
14 Dudes
15 Take things one step ___ time: 2 words
16 Sight, smell, or taste, for example
17 24-hour period
19 "This ___ outrage!": 2 words
21 Part of a molecule
23 Black-and-white whale
24 Young dog
27 Piece of gym equipment that makes you feel like you're paddling a boat: 2 words
30 Male doll in "Toy Story 3"
31 Country whose capital is Tehran
32 2008 animated film about a lab assistant
33 Goes from 10 to 11 years old, for example
34 Animal companion of Tarzan
35 Throw a baseball toward a batter
38 The ___ Woodman (character in Oz)
40 Opposite of even
43 In any ___ (no matter what)
44 Stop
45 Neither this ___ that
46 ___ Wilder (actor who once played Willy Wonka)
47 Bit of sunshine
48 Pen for pigs

DOWN

1 Meat from a pig
2 President Lincoln's nickname
3 Beginning of the evening
4 Pottery material
5 ___-O-Honey (chewy candy)
6 Piece of gym equipment that makes you feel like you're climbing the steps in a building
7 Name of the reindeer in "Frozen"
8 2,000 pounds

9 Government agency that collects taxes: Abbreviation

10 Bread that may have seeds

13 Abraham's son, in the Bible

18 "What ___ supposed to do now?": 2 words

20 Read quickly

21 Boat built by Noah

22 Tic-tac-___

23 Fairy tale monster

24 Birds you often see in city parks

25 Colorful card game

26 Miles ___ gallon

28 When the moon is visible

29 Cool and modern

33 Annoying skin condition

34 Raggedy ___ (boy doll)

35 Wooden target in ringtoss

36 "What a fool ___ been!"

37 Two fewer than a dozen

39 Every once ___ while: 2 words

41 Decimal point or period

42 As exciting as watching paint ___

ACROSS

1 Something to drink out of

4 Does a performance

8 Raisin ___ (type of cereal)

12 Sick ___ dog: 2 words

13 One of the colors on the American flag

14 Road ___ (anger felt by a driver)

15 Party game where you try to grab a seat: 2 words

18 Devours

19 Barbed ___ fence

20 A goalie plays in front of it

21 "Tra ___" (sounds in a song): 2 words

23 Miles ___ gallon

24 "That is correct"

25 Flow back from the shore

27 Half of twenty

29 Half of a pair of pants

32 "Are you a good witch ___ bad witch?" (line in "The Wizard of Oz"): 2 words

34 Fuzzy thing you wear on the foot

37 Fourth month of the year: Abbreviation

38 Moving trucks

40 How Dumbledore would say "Unfortunately ..."

42 Party game where you try to collect various things: 2 words

45 "The Wizard of Oz" dog

46 ___ Lovato (pop singer)

47 Sense of self-worth

48 Meat-and-potatoes meal

49 Stumble on the ice

50 Cutting tool

DOWN

1 "Which ___ first, the chicken or the egg?"

2 Typical

3 Spaghetti or macaroni, for example

4 Start of the alphabet

5 What a cat scratches with

6 Flower from the Netherlands

7 Something that might be whispered

8 Garment similar to a bikini top

9 Like weather when you'd use an umbrella

10 Have the same opinion

11 Birds build them in trees

16 Small spot of land in an ocean

17 "___ the thing ..." ("Let me explain ...")

22 "Up ___ the world so high ..." (lyric in "Twinkle, Twinkle Little Star")

26 Puts a mark on cattle

28 Man in the Bible who built an ark

29 Sticks around for a long time

30 Theme park at Walt Disney World

31 Shred, like a hard cheese

33 Devil's opposite

35 Crossword hints

36 Large female animal in "Winnie-the-Pooh"

39 Prefix meaning "half"

41 Pack away

43 Solemn promise

44 Tear roughly

10

ACROSS

1 Containers for jelly
5 Large storage tank
8 Just ___ (not very many): 2 words
12 State whose capital is Salt Lake City
13 Ginger ___ (bubbly drink)
14 Have a ___ to eat
15 Opening in a fence
16 Los Angeles's state: Abbreviation
17 Less than twice
18 Largest continent on earth
20 Not quiet
22 Foldaway bed for a camper
24 Genetic material: Abbreviation
26 Circus clown's leg-lengthening pole
29 "Get off the stage!"
30 Room that's just under the roof
32 "This is neither the time ___ the place"
33 "Please be quiet!"
35 "Is it a boy ___ girl?": 2 words
36 "Family ___" (animated comedy)
37 Music player made by Apple
39 Pump ___ (lift weights)
41 White as a ghost
43 "Six-pack" muscles
45 Presidential power to kill a bill
48 Rod that connects truck wheels
49 Make a knot
50 End of a prayer
51 Dandelion, for example
52 Website pop-ups
53 The ___ Star State (nickname for Texas)

DOWN

1 Large container for bleach
2 ___ loss for words (speechless): 2 words
3 Pixar movie about a rodent who wanted to be a chef
4 Contraction meaning "that woman is"
5 Empty, like a hotel room
6 Apple pie ___ mode: 2 words
7 Show and ___ (classroom activity)
8 "I've got a bad feeling ___ this"
9 Pixar movie about a lost fish: 2 words
10 Abbreviation that follows a list of things

11 "___ Willie Winkie" (nursery rhyme)

19 State whose capital is Boise

21 "Sesame Street" grouch

22 TV network where you'd see "Survivor" and "The Amazing Race": Abbreviation

23 ___ and aah (sound impressed)

25 From ___ Z (completely): 2 words

27 "Skip to My ___"

28 Make an attempt

31 Eye parts that contain the pupils

34 Drive too fast

38 Information for a computer

40 The ___ Office (room in the White House)

41 Hound's hand

42 A hatchet is a small one

44 Try to win something at an auction

46 Number that is often at the top of a ranking scale

47 Number that is often at the bottom of a ranking scale

ACROSS

1 Earn an acceptable grade
5 Sedans and convertibles
9 What Bart Simpson rides to school
12 Door that you leave through
13 Unruly crowd situation
14 "If you have any questions, just ___"
15 "Wish you ___ here"
16 Annual celebration that involves planting trees: 2 words
18 Network that hands out Video Music Awards and Movie Awards: Abbreviation
20 Girl lamb
21 Member of the police force
24 Single part of a set of exercises
26 Truth or ___ (party game)
30 Annual celebration that honors American leaders: 2 words
34 Pasta sauce brand
35 Every ___ and then (once in a while)
36 It can hide gray hair
37 What a cow says
40 Actor Hanks who does the voice of Woody in "Toy Story"
42 Annual celebration for workers: 2 words
46 Gorillas, for example
50 ___ cream sandwich
51 Ending for "million" or "billion"
52 Rescue
53 Teacher's ___ (favorite student)
54 Opposite of right
55 Slow-cooked meal

DOWN

1 Long bench in a church
2 Lumberjack's tool
3 "Aye, aye, ___!"
4 Long, slender part of a cherry
5 Had a serious longing for
6 ___ conditioner
7 It might be worn over pajamas
8 Put away, like carry-on luggage
9 Wicked
10 Country between Canada and Mexico: Abbreviation
11 "The ___ is falling!" (Chicken Little's warning)
17 Baseball team from Cincinnati
19 "Prefix for "pod" or "angle"

21 A lifeguard might have to perform it: Abbreviation

22 "Are you a man ___ mouse?": 2 words

23 Wooden pin in a coatrack

25 It might have a rollerball or a felt tip

27 Calculate a sum

28 Blu-___ disc

29 Bird's-___ view

31 Japanese variety of wrestling

32 "Hold your horses!": 2 words

33 Kill ___ birds with one stone

38 Verbal

39 "Garfield" dog

41 Boston's state: Abbreviation

42 ___-sync (mouth the lyrics)

43 Playing card with the letter A on it

44 Gamble

45 Sound made by Little Orphan Annie's dog

47 ___ on the back (warm gesture)

48 New Year's ___ (December 31)

49 Fasten with stitches

ACROSS

1 Corn on the ___

4 "Today I ___ man" (what a Jewish boy says at his bar mitzvah): 2 words

7 ___ and tell (school activity)

11 The "O" in "IOU"

12 Vehicle that often goes to airports

13 Musical instrument played by Lady Gaga

14 What Frisbees and beach balls are made of

16 Creature from outer space

17 "Once ___ a time ..."

18 Bad smell

19 Where the bride and groom say "I do"

21 Vehicle that might be a double-decker

22 Not wet

25 Inlets of the sea that are smaller than gulfs

26 Pizza ___ (fast food chain)

27 Opposite of false

28 Fruit Roll-___ (chewy snacks)

29 Consume

30 People who write verses

31 "Don't get carried ___"

33 Popular songs

34 Tools used for manicuring nails

36 First book of the Bible

39 Material in walrus tusks

40 School class where you might make a collage

41 Alter ___ (secret identity)

42 Tina and Louise's brother on "Bob's Burgers"

43 Zodiac sign with the shortest name

44 It's what you do "gently down the stream"

DOWN

1 Person who makes arrests

2 Bird that eats mice

3 Where you might get a cut or a dye job: 2 words

4 Movie performer

5 ___ course (entrée)

6 Start of "The Alphabet Song"

7 Storage tower on a farm

8 Person who might give you a cut or a dye job

9 Half of two

10 Word that sounds like 9-Down

13 Shoulder ___ (parts of a football uniform)
15 Relaxing resorts
18 "Get ___ of here!"
19 Monkey friend of Aladdin
20 Trip to the end of the pool and back
21 "Thanks, ___ no thanks"
23 Same old boring routine
24 What a nod might mean
26 Dry grass eaten by some farm animals
27 Large canvas bag
29 Simple

30 ___ beans (small, speckled vegetables)
32 "If I ___ King of the Forest" (song in "The Wizard of Oz")
33 In this location
34 Fruit used in Nabisco's "Newtons" cookies
35 "Now ___ seen everything!"
36 Four quarts: Abbreviation
37 "Where did ___ wrong?": 2 words
38 Female pig

ACROSS

1 Has to
5 Prepare potatoes, in a way
9 Slim ___ (brand of jerky snacks)
12 Where India and China are
13 ___ code (start of a phone number)
14 Top card in poker
15 Job that involves hammers and saws
17 Ping-Pong table divider
18 Have dinner
19 Prefix for "finals" or "formal"
21 Task
24 Prime ___ (type of steak)
26 Smooth bedsheet material
29 Snug as a bug in ___: 2 words
31 What a magician uses to cut someone in half
33 Bird that symbolizes peace
34 Liquid in a dog's bowl
36 Father
38 Color of Superman's cape
39 Coagulate, like blood
41 "Help us, we're sinking!"
43 "___, humbug!" (Scrooge's shout)
45 Job that involves blueprints and rulers

50 "When I was your ___ ..."
51 Mound on the beach
52 "Dear ___ Hansen"
53 Word typically used with "neither"
54 Button to press when you're done writing an email
55 Took a turn in a game

DOWN

1 ___ and cheese (pasta dish)
2 Country whose anthem is "The Star-Spangled Banner": Abbreviation
3 Gentleman's title
4 Masking ___
5 Praying ___ (type of insect)
6 Sculptures, paintings, and so on
7 Catches sight of
8 Animals similar to rabbits
9 Job that involves brooms and mops
10 Break the ___ (get the conversation going)
11 "As I was going to St. Ives, I ___ a man with seven wives ..."
16 Place for a hearing aid

20 Humor magazine that features "Spy vs. Spy"
21 Lower part of the face
22 "Are you a man ___ Muppet?" (question in the movie "The Muppets"): 2 words
23 Job that involves meat and knives
25 Go from ___ to worse
27 "___ changed my mind"
28 Mr. Flanders on "The Simpsons"
30 Gooey stuff that holds hair in place
32 Cleaned up

35 Streets
37 "Where ___ start?": 2 words
40 "Based on a ___ story"
42 Meat-and-potatoes dish
43 Ray-___ (brand of sunglasses)
44 Long ___ (way back when)
46 Cable channel that focuses on current events: Abbreviation
47 Night before a big holiday
48 Soda container
49 Powerful explosive: Abbreviation

ACROSS

1 Fresh ___ daisy: 2 words
4 School support organization: Abbreviation
7 Flat bread that has a pocket
11 Squirt ___ (water pistol)
12 Sprinted
13 Father of Cain and Abel, in the Bible
14 Jedi Master who helped teach Luke Skywalker, in the "Star Wars" movies: 2 words
17 Month when Mother's Day is
18 Sara ___ (brand of frozen desserts)
19 Dr. Seuss character who speaks for the trees
22 Stuff that can make hair spiky
23 Cheerful character in "Inside Out"
26 Spoken
27 "Let me ___ it this way ..."
28 What a dog might bury in the yard
29 Valuable stone
30 "Crime does not ___"
31 Things turned when reading a book
32 What's inside a scuba tank

33 Sports team's supporter
34 Luke and Leia's mother, in the "Star Wars" movies: 2 words
40 ___ vera (soothing plant)
41 Group of Cub Scouts
42 Item in the middle of a badminton court
43 Someone between 12 and 20
44 Tight ___ (football position)
45 What Oz's Tin Man carried

DOWN

1 Some time ___ (back in the past)
2 Underwater warship, for short
3 Beast
4 Say grace before a meal, for example
5 Color of coffee ice cream
6 Sock that barely covers the heel
7 Piece of glass in a window
8 Wedding vow: 2 words
9 You might open a new one in a web browser
10 "___ missing something?": 2 words
15 Candle drippings

16 Fish that resembles a snake
19 It's carved to make a totem pole
20 Valuable mineral
21 Los Angeles football player
22 "Family ___" (animated series on Fox)
23 Take a run around a park
24 "Give me ___ good reason!"
25 Agreeable answer
27 Where you'd see marching bands and floats

28 Yellow fruit
30 Dessert with a crust and filling
31 Mouse ___ (computer accessory)
32 "You said it, Reverend!"
33 Discover
34 "Wheel of Fortune" host Sajak
35 Ginger ___ (fizzy beverage)
36 Female fawn
37 Word on a bathroom door
38 Comic book villain Luthor
39 Gobbled down

ACROSS

1 Make happen
6 Ms. ___-Man (classic video game)
9 A violin player uses one
12 Chef's protective garment
13 A celebrity might have an inflated one
14 Weird thing seen in the sky: Abbreviation
15 Heavy-duty vehicle used on construction sites
17 Against the ___ (not legal)
18 Room that could serve as a man cave
19 Opposite of buy
21 Scientific researcher's workplace
24 Mountain ___ (soft drink)
26 A pentagon has five of them
29 "Rub-a-dub-dub, three men in ___": 2 words
31 Boar's mate
33 White bird
34 Whiter in the face
36 "Ready or ___, here I come!"
38 ___ down to business
39 People born under the sign of the Lion
41 Liquid that food is deep-fried in
43 Young dog

45 Event where a matador waves a red cape
50 "___ only as directed" (phrase on a medicine bottle)
51 Portland's state: Abbreviation
52 White, powdery ingredient used by bakers
53 Light brown
54 Prop for a golf ball
55 Covered in grime from a fireplace

DOWN

1 Taxi
2 Squishee seller on "The Simpsons"
3 Web address: Abbreviation
4 Auctioneer's cry while banging a gavel
5 Stopped
6 Candy in a flip-back dispenser
7 Numbers on birthday cards
8 Uneaten parts of apples
9 Canine with a wrinkly face
10 "Tales ___ Fourth Grade Nothing" (Judy Blume novel): 2 words

11 "That's amazing!"
16 Dollar bills featuring George Washington
20 Flip your ___ (lose self-control)
21 Where a kid sits for a photo with Santa
22 Take things one day ___ time: 2 words
23 Where relief pitchers warm up before entering a baseball game
25 Didn't lose
27 Christmas ___ (December 24)
28 ___ foot in (enter)
30 Honey maker

32 Material that comes from sheep
35 Wall-E, for one
37 Minor quarrels
40 Confident
42 "___ & Stitch" (Disney movie)
43 "Don't ___ words in my mouth"
44 Uncle Sam's country: Abbreviation
46 First name that can be used by a boy or a girl
47 Sticky gunk
48 Crude house you might find on a desert island
49 Attempt

ACROSS

1 Lousy
4 Recordings that could be "ripped" or "burned": Abbreviation
7 Person who flies a plane
12 "You've got a brain. ___ it!"
13 One way to eat carrots
14 Big sports stadium
15 Crayola color
16 "What ___ doing here?": 2 words
17 ___ Tots (fried potato puffs)
18 Iron ___ (Tony Stark's alter ego)
20 Slender
22 What trees provide on a sunny day
24 "If I Ran the ___" (Dr. Seuss book)
25 ___ and arrow (archer's equipment)
28 What headphones cover
29 747, for one
30 "The Empire Strikes Back" princess
31 "___ a stupid question, get a stupid answer"
32 Something in a garage
33 Wishing ___ (things you might throw coins into)
34 Werewolf's sound
35 Greedy person
36 Material in a wedding dress, often
39 Feasted on
41 Ending for "child" or "fool"
44 Opposite of dead
45 Neither here ___ there
46 Colorful card game with Skip and Reverse cards
47 Uses a paper towel on
48 It could change a blonde to a brunette
49 Trim the grass

DOWN

1 "Close, ___ no cigar"
2 Busy ___ bee: 2 words
3 European country whose capital is Copenhagen
4 Big machine that lifts a wrecking ball
5 Barrier in a river
6 European country whose capital is Bern
7 Backyard barbecue place
8 Country that borders Afghanistan and Pakistan
9 "___ It Go" ("Frozen" song)
10 "Don't put all your eggs in ___ basket"

11 Road-repairing material
19 Commercial interruptions
21 Very spicy
22 The Mediterranean ___
23 "The tribe ___ spoken" ("Survivor" line)
25 European country whose capital is Brussels
26 Stuff that comes out of the ground in a gusher
27 "That ___ a close one!"
29 Bone that moves when you chew

30 Zodiac sign for most August babies
32 Edible ice cream holders
33 "___ the Wild Things Are" (Maurice Sendak book)
34 Bees live in it
36 Tool with teeth
37 "___ Baba and the Forty Thieves"
38 "Take a ___ from me ..."
40 Item in Santa's sack
42 ___-cone (frosty treat)
43 "___ to Train Your Dragon"

ACROSS

1 ___ Ketchum ("Pokémon" hero)
4 Throw the dice
8 ___ and ends (miscellaneous items)
12 Drink made by Tetley and Lipton
13 Cookie with a Double Stuf variety
14 Any object seen in a play
15 Sea creatures like Ariel
17 Not difficult
18 Get ___ of (throw out)
19 "Monsters, ___" (Pixar movie)
20 Picks up the check
22 Unit of power used for light bulbs
25 Have
28 Program on a smartphone
29 What the IRS collects from workers
30 "Mr. Brown Can ___! Can You?" (Dr. Seuss book)
31 "The Lion," in astrology
32 Garden in the Old Testament
33 Bones that are right above the neck
34 Most common word in English

36 Fuel that flows through pipelines
37 Place on the Internet
39 Tallest animals on earth
44 Under's opposite
45 ___-friendly (easy to operate)
46 "I ___ it all to my parents"
47 Geeky person
48 Treasure hunters follow them
49 "Are we there ___?"

DOWN

1 Cash-dispensing device: Abbreviation
2 Visualize
3 Hogwarts boy who was in Gryffindor: 2 words
4 "Follow the Yellow Brick ___"
5 "Either you do it ___ will!": 2 words
6 Had followers
7 ___ Angeles, California
8 Unlocked
9 Hogwarts boy who was in Slytherin: 2 words
10 Spanish for "two"
11 Undercover agent

16 Prefix for "spell" or "behaving"
19 "Don't judge a book by ___ cover"
20 Good buddy
21 Chimpanzee, for one
22 Crumpled-up mass of paper
23 A tomahawk is a small one
24 Fifty divided by five
26 "That's astonishing!"
27 Negative answers
29 Thin, short-sleeved shirt
33 Brand of peanut butter

35 Group of cattle
36 Lifeboat paddles
37 Like father, like ___
38 "___ Been Working on the Railroad"
39 Candy that comes in packs
40 "This ___ rip-off!": 2 words
41 Democrat's counterpart in politics: Abbreviation
42 Farm animal that sounds like "you"
43 Complete collection

ACROSS

1 Trail
5 Use a phone
9 Short snooze
12 Unit of farmland
13 Neighborhood
14 ___ Direction (popular boy band)
15 Astronaut who was the first person on the moon: 2 words
18 Center of a peach
19 Small thing that's planted in a garden
20 Raccoon's foot
23 "Haven't we ___ before?"
25 Chief Wiggum's son on "The Simpsons"
28 "I have ___ feeling about this": 2 words
30 Young friend of Winnie-the-Pooh
32 Princess who said this: "Help me, Obi-Wan Kenobi. You're my only hope."
33 Places where you can buy fresh meat
35 Major-league athlete
37 "Ready, ___, go!"
38 Touches on the shoulder
40 Small dog that was originally bred in China
42 Astronaut in the "Toy Story" movies: 2 words

48 "I could ___ a hand"
49 Imaginative concept
50 Female horse
51 ___-guzzler (car that needs lots of fuel)
52 Person who is almost an adult
53 "___ right up!" (carnival barker's shout)

DOWN

1 "Peter ___" (Disney movie)
2 You might play a two on it, in solitaire
3 Prefix that means "three"
4 Give assistance to
5 Jimmy ___ (American president in the 1970s)
6 Where the elbow and wrist are
7 "I couldn't care ___"
8 In a little while
9 Strands of pasta
10 Raggedy ___ (doll with red hair)
11 Like a square ___ in a round hole (not really fitting)
16 Word that comes between "ready" and "fire"
17 Not artificial

20 Lily ___ (something a frog sits on)

21 President Lincoln's nickname

22 Dances that are often done to classical music

24 Big ___ (circus tent)

26 "Four and twenty blackbirds baked in a ___"

27 Sombrero or beret, for example

29 Cameron ___ (actress who voiced Fiona in "Shrek")

31 Child without parents

34 Banana ___ (ice cream treat)

36 "For crying ___ loud!"

39 Get up on the wrong ___ of the bed

41 Places where people work out

42 Insect

43 Country whose anthem is "The Star-Spangled Banner": Abbreviation

44 "___ whiz!"

45 Have breakfast

46 "___ you crazy?"

47 One part of a set of exercises

ACROSS

1 The whole shooting ___ (everything)
6 "Flattery will ___ you nowhere"
9 Lock opener
12 How to say "hello" in Honolulu
13 Ginger ___ (bubbly beverage)
14 "___ little teapot, short and stout ...": 2 words
15 Transparent
16 Arranged in a row: 2 words
18 "___ me about it!"
20 Sandpaper's color
21 60-minute periods: Abbreviation
24 Cries loudly
26 What you try to get in musical chairs
29 This one and that one
31 Prince ___ (Aladdin's other identity, in "Aladdin")
32 Use a computer keyboard
33 Slim, black woodwind instrument
34 Confused state
36 Have a look
37 Married woman's title: Abbreviation
39 Out of battery power
41 Made really big cuts in

44 From the capital of Italy
48 ___-Man (video game character who chomps dots)
49 "___ never heard of such a thing!"
50 Copy with a pencil
51 ___ Wednesday (winter holiday)
52 Pay-___-view
53 Didn't like at all

DOWN

1 Big ___ (fast-food burger)
2 100%
3 Big ___ (body part that could be stubbed)
4 Make small talk
5 Animals that are a lot like rabbits
6 Organ of the body that stores bile from the liver
7 ___ Manning (quarterback who was the Super Bowl MVP twice)
8 Pup ___ (small outdoor shelter)
9 Organs of the body that filter the blood
10 Ostrich's Australian relative

11 Sound like a small, annoying dog

17 Direction of the rising sun

19 Take a ___ off (sit down)

21 Cable channel that's run "Sesame Street" since 2016: Abbreviation

22 Baseball commissioner Manfred

23 Organ of the body that helps digest food

25 How big something is

27 Animal companion of Tarzan

28 Shirt bought as a souvenir

30 His and ___

35 This planet

38 The Titanic, for one

40 "___ the Explorer"

41 Place to be pampered

42 ___ Vegas, Nevada

43 Adam and ___

45 Rug on a bathroom floor

46 Top card in the game of war

47 Father of Rod and Todd on "The Simpsons"

ACROSS

1 Performs in a skit
5 Groundhog ___ (February 2)
8 Animal that followed the Pied Piper
11 Cleansing bar found in the shower
12 Ginger ___ (soda choice)
13 In this day and ___ (nowadays)
14 "Dr." or "USA," for example
17 Jazz horn, for short
18 Egg-laying bird on a farm
19 ___ standstill (not moving): 2 words
22 Amounts given to waiters
25 Cain's brother, in the Bible
28 Connect the ___ (activity involving drawing lines)
30 Kid in a stroller
31 Change your address
32 Bottom of a sandal
33 Line formed when stitching together two pieces of cloth
35 Drenched
36 What "&" represents

38 Not cooked
40 "Don't" and "I'm," for example
46 Insect living in a hill
47 Timeline segment
48 Ark builder in the Bible
49 Afternoon beverage in England
50 "Charlotte's ___"
51 Perimeter

DOWN

1 Gentle ___ lamb: 2 words
2 Uneaten part of an ear of corn
3 Small flaps on file folders
4 "Jack ___ could eat no fat ..."
5 "Captain Underpants" author Pilkey
6 Boxing Hall of Famer Muhammad
7 Opposite of "nope"
8 There's supposedly a pot of gold at the end of it
9 Many moons ___ (a long time back)
10 The first two-digit number

15 Ways to leave a highway
16 Group of athletes
19 What "words from our sponsor" are
20 ___ close for comfort
21 The capital of Georgia
23 Edgar Allan ___ (spooky author)
24 Begin
26 Wall-E's love interest
27 Grant permission to
29 Dropped in the mail

34 State whose capital is Augusta
37 Made a picture
39 Material used by carpenters
40 Adult kitten
41 Number of horns on a unicorn
42 "___ we there yet?"
43 Uber alternative
44 Pester constantly
45 Feminine pronoun

ACROSS

1 Stay in a tent in the wilderness
5 Defrost
9 The ___ Heel State (nickname for North Carolina)
12 General location
13 Speed contest
14 "What else could ___?": 2 words
15 Billionaire who was one of the founders of Microsoft: 2 words
17 "___ Bless America"
18 "Don't ___ it get you down"
19 "___ got a bad feeling about this!"
20 Over in that spot
22 Suffix for "host" or "lion"
23 Cincinnati's pro baseball team
25 Cookie you can twist apart to eat the filling
26 "That's ___, folks!" (line from Porky Pig)
27 Chicken drumstick
29 Young deer
32 What a sunflower grows from
34 Things you might frame and hang on a wall

37 By yourself
39 ___ out (take it easy)
40 Garden tool for breaking up soil
41 Poorly lit
42 Billionaire who was one of the founders of Apple: 2 words
45 Adam's mate in the Garden of Eden
46 Tree with green needles
47 "That makes ___ of sense": 2 words
48 Family room
49 Safety devices for high-wire walkers
50 Applies water to

DOWN

1 Very thick wire
2 Astrology's sign of the Ram
3 Goes from solid to liquid
4 Friend
5 Goes from country to country
6 Despised
7 Card that might beat a king
8 The Wicked Witch of the ___
9 Large, striped cat

10 Love a lot

11 Competition with roping and riding

16 Young lady

21 Plump pig

24 Parts of a shirt that cover the arms

26 Raggedy ___ doll

28 Outer border

29 Lost color over time

30 Still breathing

31 Ladies

33 In any ___ (no matter what)

34 "There's ___ in the Bucket" (kids' song): 2 words

35 Something that's similar to an android

36 Examinations

38 TV channel that focuses on athletics: Abbreviation

43 Score where neither team is ahead

44 Part of the face where the chin is

22

ACROSS

1 Not wild, like an animal
5 It can show you how to get around
8 Requests
12 Continent connected to Europe
13 ___-surf (search your own name online)
14 Person who writes rhymes
15 ___, present, and future
16 Flotsam or Jetsam in "The Little Mermaid," for example
17 Small and weak
18 Chair
20 Final
22 Carnivals
24 Female bird on a farm
25 Item worn on the head
28 "___ a small world after all ..."
29 Object
31 Do-or-___ situation
32 Oxygen or helium, for example
33 ___ cord (line that's attached to a parachute)
34 South American relative of the camel
36 Apple's mobile music player
38 Hide and ___ (kids' game)
39 Ready to be harvested and eaten
41 Decimal point
43 Ditch around a castle
46 Bratty little kids
47 Lamb's mother
48 Sergeant Snorkel's dog in "Beetle Bailey"
49 Something that attracts a fish to a hook
50 ___ Hampshire
51 Cary, Gary, or Mary

DOWN

1 Water faucet
2 Busy ___ beaver: 2 words
3 State where Elvis Presley was born
4 "Peter, Peter, pumpkin ___ ..."
5 Make ends ___ (get by financially)
6 How old someone is
7 Flower substance that many people are allergic to
8 Droid or iPhone programs
9 State where Mount Rushmore is: 2 words
10 Barbie's guy

11 Pig's pen

19 George Jetson's pet dog

21 It can be measured with a protractor, in math class

22 ___ leaves (what Adam and Eve wore)

23 Move ___ snail's pace: 2 words

24 Word that's said twice before "Hooray!"

26 Prepare to shoot

27 Beverage that may be served hot or iced

30 Concealed

35 Flavor of a yellow Life Saver

37 Annoying person

38 Hearty meal often containing beef

39 Chest bone that's part of a "cage"

40 "___ little teapot ...": 2 words

42 "I ___ it all to you"

44 Device where you can get $20 bills: Abbreviation

45 ___ shoes (ballerina's footwear)

ACROSS

1 State that's home to lots of Mormons
5 Mix, like paint
9 Camel's color
12 Stand like a supermodel
13 Crunchy Mexican food
14 "That's disgusting!"
15 Chain that specializes in coffee
17 Hair salon's styling goo
18 Piece of furniture used mainly at night
19 Cry really hard
21 TV show interruptions
24 Person who's not telling the truth
27 Opposite of "yep"
30 Chain that specializes in pizza: 2 words
33 "Don't get the wrong ___"
34 Texting button
35 Highest point
36 Tool for cutting firewood
38 What tailors do
40 Male sheep
42 Chain that specializes in hamburgers
48 "I ___ you big-time!" ("I'm very grateful")
49 Badly injure
50 Toy that's maneuvered with one hand: Hyphenated
51 Got married
52 Gorillas and chimpanzees
53 Hearty meal in a bowl

DOWN

1 "Life has its ___ and downs"
2 Preschooler
3 Thin ___ rail: 2 words
4 Flavoring such as mint or parsley
5 Social ___ (school subject)
6 Tic-___-toe
7 "Yuck!"
8 Betsy ___ (legendary flagmaker)
9 Harbor vessel that tows ships
10 "Act your ___ and not your shoe size!"
11 Sports group that awards the Stanley Cup: Abbreviation
16 Liberty ___ (Philadelphia landmark)
20 Slip-___ (shoes without laces)
21 ___ Baba
22 Accomplished
23 Cooked over boiling water

25 Blackjack card worth one or eleven

26 Amounts asked for by kidnappers

28 Person who gets paid to play sports

29 Supposed ability to read people's thoughts: Abbreviation

31 Luxury ___ (square on a Monopoly board)

32 Where the first humans were, according to the Bible

37 Actress Watson who played Hermione Granger

39 Methods

40 Line of chairs in a theater

41 "I'm in ___!" ("That was amazing!")

43 "Stuck a feather in his ___ and called it macaroni" ("Yankee Doodle" lyric)

44 One of five in a Yahtzee set

45 Parking area

46 What's used to color fabrics

47 She-pig

ACROSS

1 Smartphone purchases
5 Baby's dinnertime covering
8 Performs in the theater
12 What you're reading right now
13 "___ you listening to me?"
14 Part of the lower leg
15 Middle ___ (where Saudi Arabia and Israel are)
16 Potato chip container
17 Captain America, for one
18 Bro's sibling
19 Freak out during an emergency
21 Mend with needle and thread
22 More pleasant
24 ___ Ark (boat in the Bible)
26 Prefix for "violent" or "sense"
27 Boxer Muhammad ___
28 Steak shaped like a letter: Hyphenated
30 The American flag has fifty of them
32 Half of four
33 Pulls hard, like a rope
35 Body part with a lobe and a drum

37 Mob scene in the streets
39 Come ___ screeching halt: 2 words
40 Facial problem for many teenagers
41 Vanish ___ thin air
42 Word ending that means "most"
43 Animals that hang upside down in caves
44 "Ramona the ___" (Beverly Cleary book)
45 Dark-colored type of bread
46 Number on a baseball card, for short

DOWN

1 Cards without numbers or faces on them
2 Like a pizza with no toppings
3 Feline who appears in "Shrek 2": 3 words
4 "I had my heart ___ on it"
5 Elephant king in a series of books
6 "If ___ the Circus" (Dr. Seuss book): 2 words
7 Get started

8 Campfire residue

9 Feline who appears in "Alice in Wonderland": 2 words

10 Cars have four of them

11 Stuff shoveled in winter

19 Cent

20 Layers of paint

23 Dove's sound

25 Apple pie ___ mode: 2 words

28 Strong string around a package

29 "Peter Peter Pumpkin ___" (nursery rhyme)

30 What to do in a roller rink

31 He brings presents on Christmas

32 Round-___ ticket

34 Like a person who asks a lot of personal questions

36 Take it easy for a bit

38 Tater ___ (fried potato morsel)

40 Stomach muscles

ACROSS

1 Type of dancing that's noisy
4 Large shopping center
8 ___ and pans
12 "This ___ job for Superman!": 2 words
13 Cookie sometimes used in cheesecakes
14 Zone
15 Spice that's used on toast and apples
17 "This little piggy ___ to market ..."
18 Clip-___ (easy-to-attach earrings)
19 Criminal group
21 Shirts and blouses
24 "Can't we all just ___ along?"
25 Playing card that beats a king
28 Needle ___ haystack: 2 words
29 "In what place?"
31 Right this minute
32 Miles ___ hour
33 Long, wriggly fish
34 "Here today, ___ tomorrow"
35 Root beer or ginger ale, for example
37 "Seen ___ good movies lately?"
39 Hairless

41 Herb that's also a girl's name
46 Got on in years
47 Musical threesome
48 Pool player's stick
49 Balls and dolls, for example
50 ___ Combs (Puff Daddy's given name)
51 Letters on some explosives

DOWN

1 ___ Tac (brand of breath mints)
2 "Do ___ say!" (parent's warning): 2 words
3 Skillet
4 Sound made by someone in pain
5 Upper limbs
6 Summer zodiac sign
7 Lengthier
8 It's often moved to start a chess game
9 Herb that's often sprinkled onto pizza
10 Number of biblical commandments
11 Used a park bench
16 Negative replies
20 Enjoyed a buffet
21 Bonus for good service

22 Last number in a countdown

23 Herb that's frequently used as a garnish on a plate

24 Type of toothpaste or hair product

26 ___ artist (scammer)

27 Mother with little lambs

29 Day before Thursday: Abbreviation

30 Valentine's Day symbols

34 Building where people lift weights

36 Chances that something will happen

37 Where China and Japan are

38 ___ Carrot (fluorescent Crayola color)

39 Animal that a vampire could turn into

40 Back in time

42 Metal in raw form

43 "Get your ___ together!"

44 Go fast on foot

45 "So near and ___ so far"

ACROSS

1 Bound with rope
5 Thick, fluffy type of carpeting
9 Disco ___ (character on "The Simpsons")
12 Hundred ___ Wood (where Winnie-the-Pooh lives)
13 "___ is but a dream" (end of "Row, Row, Row Your Boat")
14 Play on words
15 Unkind
16 Not-so-gentle giant
17 Join together
19 Nickname for a female sibling
21 "For ___ a Jolly Good Fellow"
22 Rant and ___
23 "Oh no, a mouse!"
24 "The doctor will ___ you now"
25 Concludes
28 Compact ___ player
30 Angry pit bull's sound
32 Once and for ___
34 "I think I messed up": Hyphenated
37 "This nonsense ___ got to stop!"
38 "I thought I'd ___ laughing"
39 Noise made by a sleeper
40 Dumb dog in the comics
42 Place for a pet canary
44 "We're number ___!"
45 Gets into a recliner
46 "Don't ___ think about it!"
47 "That's too funny," in a text
48 What elves make at Santa's workshop
49 Black bit in a watermelon

DOWN

1 Not wild, like house pets
2 It can cool down your drink
3 Wipe clean, like a blackboard
4 Declared to be false
5 ___-mo replay
6 You might graduate from it when you're around 18 years old: 2 words
7 "It's ___ country": 2 words
8 Birds that fly in a V formation

9 Metal attachment on a cowboy's boot
10 ___ fish sandwich
11 You might graduate from it when you're around 22 years old
18 Fifty divided by five
20 Go downhill in the snow
26 Mom and ___
27 Pieces of pizza
29 It shines in the sky

30 Halloween costume that can be made from a sheet
31 It may be "AM/FM"
33 Go away
35 "Just answer yes ___": 2 words
36 Back of the foot
39 Mail out
41 Suffix for "lion" or "count"
43 "Gosh!"

ACROSS

1 Head coverings
5 "___ me if I care"
8 "Love ___ neighbor"
11 Sound of a sneeze
13 ___ rummy (card game)
14 "___ Willie Winkie"
15 Not moving
16 Oxygen or hydrogen, for example
18 Enjoy a book or magazine
20 Peachy ___ (nifty)
21 Little kid
23 Animal's body hair
25 Another name for the devil
28 Techniques
30 Play-___ (modeling clay)
32 Use a keyboard
33 Proposal
35 A messy eater might use one
37 Not very many
38 Dr. Frankenstein's assistant
40 "Star Wars: The Last ___"
42 Ingredient in a Snickers or Twix
45 Couches
48 Grown-___ (adults)
49 President Lincoln's nickname
50 Name of a movie or song
51 "Thanks, ___ no thanks"
52 Horse that's past its prime
53 Defrost in the microwave

DOWN

1 "The emperor ___ no clothes"
2 "You need to clean up your ___!"
3 Day in October when Halloween is: Hyphenated
4 Bottom of a sneaker
5 Get older
6 Fabric produced by worms
7 Leg joints
8 Day in December when Christmas is: Hyphenated
9 Rooster's mate
10 "I haven't decided ___" ("Ask me later")
12 "Frozen" snowman
17 What vegetarians don't eat
19 Firecracker that fizzles

21 Number of items in a pair

22 Big doofus

24 Alternative nickname for Bobby

26 Large, hairy animal in a jungle

27 "Out with the old, in with the ___!"

29 Sonic the Hedgehog's company

31 Letters between G and K

34 From the biggest city in Italy

36 Opposite of worst

39 Country singer McEntire

41 "You can ___!" (encouraging remark): 2 words

42 Baby tiger

43 Convenience store proprietor on "The Simpsons"

44 One of a tripod's three supports

46 ___ mode (with ice cream on top): 2 words

47 Do some quilting

28

ACROSS

1 ___ Wednesday (time that comes before Easter)

4 Movie comedian Sandler

8 "I'll ___ and I'll puff and I'll blow your house down"

12 Black-eyed ___ (small vegetable)

13 Ice cream holder's shape

14 Where Iran and Iraq are

15 Utensil used for frying

16 Gymnastics maneuver where the feet are higher than the head

18 "___, a deer, a female deer ..."

20 Kick the bucket

21 "American ___" (music show on TV)

23 ___ eagle (American symbol)

25 A witch might wear a pointy one

28 Ear-splitting

29 Seeing ___ dog

30 Two of a kind, like gloves

31 Cover a ___ of ground

32 Finishes decorating, as a cupcake

33 Raggedy ___ (boy doll)

34 "___ scale from 1 to 10 ...": 2 words

35 Tally up

36 Cops put them on prisoners' wrists

41 Make illegal

44 Apple's digital music player

45 Hide and ___

46 "When I was your ___ ..."

47 Long benches in church

48 Wool-bearing females

49 "You have ___ to be kidding me!"

DOWN

1 iPhone purchase

2 Large body of salt water

3 Anything the teacher passes to the students

4 Dull pain

5 "I can't ___ thing with my hair!": 2 words

6 Raggedy ___ (girl doll)

7 Interferes

8 Really despise

9 Main Street, ___ (Disneyland section)

10 Part of a shark that sticks out above the water

11 Short-lived craze

17 Bad kid next door in "Toy Story"

19 Like a great-grandparent

21 "How Far ___ Go" (song in "Moana")

22 Cock-a-doodle-___ (rooster's cry)

23 "Why?" response

24 How a pirate says "yes"

25 Purse

26 Band-___ (brand of bandages)

27 "You'll never know unless you ___"

30 Soft surface to use a computer mouse on

32 "Monsters, ___" (2001 movie)

34 Chances of winning

35 Inquires

36 ___-hop (rapper's genre)

37 Hairy animal without a tail

38 At this time

39 Barely any

40 Charge for a service

42 Some time ___ (back in the past)

43 It's in the exact middle of a tennis court

ACROSS

1 Feel some soreness
5 Sunrise
9 Piece of footwear
10 One of the five Great Lakes
11 Be in debt to
14 Hit with the foot
15 Heaven-___ (miraculous)
16 "The Princess and the ___" (fairy tale)
17 Australian animal with wings
18 Ballpoint, for example
19 Fragrance
21 ___ Moines, Iowa
22 ___ and crafts
24 "A Bug's Life" bugs
25 Half a quart
27 Water faucets
29 ___ Man (member of the Avengers)
31 "It has to be ___ to be believed"
33 Easter ___ hunt
36 Stones
38 Was ahead in a contest
39 Male equivalent of "ma'am"
40 Note written by someone in debt
41 Light on a bedside table
43 Molten rock from an erupting volcano
44 Avenues and roads: Abbreviation
45 Cain's brother, in the Bible
46 Prayer conclusion
47 Like 24-karat gold
48 Curve in the road

DOWN

1 Frequently ___ questions (what "FAQ" stands for)
2 Wind ___ (tinkly device that hangs outside)
3 Magical phrase said by a professional magician: 2 words
4 "Yikes, a spider!"
5 Large, hot, sandy places
6 "___ you ashamed of yourself?"
7 Get a blue ribbon
8 Brooklyn NBA team
11 Magical phrase said by Ali Baba: 2 words
12 Past tense of "go"

13 Has a sandwich, maybe
18 Cookware item used to make omelets
20 Soda bottle top
23 Highest part of a church
26 Liquid in a ballpoint
28 Now ___ then (sometimes)
29 Bluish-purple flower
30 Get to the ___ of the problem
32 ___ Fudd (Looney Tunes character)
34 "I've been ___ a second chance"
35 Word that can go before piano or Canyon
37 Sound of a high-five
42 Pet monkey in the movie "Aladdin"
43 Science classroom

ACROSS

1 Nickname for Theodore
4 Near to the ground
7 Smooth material used in wedding gowns
12 Skating on thin ___
13 "Thanks! I ___ you one!"
14 "... to fetch her poor dog ___": 2 words
15 European capital where Big Ben is: 2 words
18 Spinning toys
19 It's revealed by your birth date
20 Rotates
22 James Bond is one
23 Person who chases criminals
26 ___ Coast (states from Maine to Florida)
27 Spanish for "two"
28 Pepsi-___
29 Insect that lives in a colony
30 "The ___ and the Hound" (Disney movie)
31 Trick-or-treating loot
32 Watched
33 "Stop right there!"
34 European capital where a famous wall used to be: 2 words
40 Hang around for

41 "What ___ you waiting for?"
42 Sound made by a dove
43 It comes between "ninth" and "eleventh"
44 Divine being
45 Number of people needed to work a seesaw

DOWN

1 "Shop ___ you drop"
2 Prefix that means "friendly to the earth"
3 Person who fills cavities
4 Froot ___ (breakfast cereal)
5 Has possession of
6 Very tiny
7 Like pants that are hanging down too much
8 "Let us know if you're ___ to attend"
9 One ___ customer: 2 words
10 Cozy place for an overnight traveler
11 Next-door neighbor of Homer and Marge
16 "___ bet on it!"
17 Takes a snooze on the sofa, maybe

20 "There are plenty of other fish in the ___"

21 Device you use when you're trying to find gold in a river

22 Chicago White ___ (baseball team)

23 Get in touch with

24 "How ___ are you now?" (birthday question)

25 Settle the bill

27 Opposite of up

28 Peaceful

30 Confidence

31 Gave a darn

32 Narrow cut in a skirt

33 The person who fights the villain

34 Black animal that lives in a cave

35 White animal that lives on a farm

36 Went for a jog

37 Palindromic word that means "joke"

38 "This instant!"

39 "___-hoo!" (attention-seeking yell)

ACROSS

1 "Please help us!"
4 "___ your money where your mouth is!"
7 Adorable
11 By ___ means necessary
12 "Oh, I figured it out!"
13 Boat that requires paddling
14 Emerald or ruby, for example
15 Kitchen container that holds a sweetener: 2 words
17 Take a ___ (wash up)
19 ___ and don'ts
20 Be very fond of
22 What a dog lifts when it's told to "Shake!"
23 Bed for an extra hotel guest
26 Scrabble piece
27 Mother
28 Circle over a saint's head
29 Pop-up ___ (internet annoyances)
30 Awful
31 Good with tools
32 ___ Antonio, Texas
33 ___ fault with (criticize)
34 Kitchen container that holds sweet snacks: 2 words
38 Researcher's workplace
41 Planet's path around the sun
42 Card that might be hidden up a cheater's sleeve
43 Bird's-___ view
44 Sit tight
45 "Indeed"
46 "I don't ___ the difference"

DOWN

1 Become droopy
2 Nine minus eight
3 Things like &, #, and %
4 Glue
5 "Nope": Hyphenated
6 Freeze ___ (schoolyard game)
7 Taxis
8 Game where you don't want a Wild Draw 4 card played on you
9 Rescue for a broken-down car
10 "Electric" fish
13 Bird that's similar to a raven
16 Eve's companion in the Garden of Eden

18 "___ you listening to me?"

20 ___ later date (not yet): 2 words

21 "Why ___ the chicken cross the road?"

22 Pea container

23 You light them on a birthday cake

24 Up there in years

25 Something to play with

27 Hair around a lion's face

28 "Star Wars" pilot ___ Solo

30 Worm on a fishhook

31 Gives a job to

32 Short play

33 Look directly at

34 Animal with an udder

35 "Are you a good witch ___ bad witch?" (question in "The Wizard of Oz"): 2 words

36 ___-Wan Kenobi

37 Blue bird

39 "Yes," to sailors

40 Pollen-collecting bug

ACROSS

1 Walked through shallow water

6 Individual serving of butter

9 ___-tac-toe (simple game)

12 "Look ___!" ("Pay attention!")

13 "___ got to tell you something ..."

14 Miss Teen ___ (annual pageant)

15 Number of days in a week

16 Container for paint or soup

17 Nibble

19 Moved fast

20 Competes in a slalom race

21 If everything goes right: 2 words

23 Baseball hit that gets the batter to third base

25 Número ___ (#1, in Spanish)

26 "Where do ___ from here?": 2 words

27 It contains an actor's lines

30 Head ___ (person in charge)

33 Single sheet in a book

34 Cable channel that shows a lot of movies: Abbreviation

36 Just a hop, ___, and jump away

37 ___ change (job for a mechanic)

38 Word that can go after straw, rasp, or blue

40 New Year's ___ (December 31)

41 "Is it a boy ___ girl?": 2 words

42 Remove a mistake, in a way

43 One plus two plus three plus four

44 "That's neither here ___ there"

45 They determine your height and hair color, for example

DOWN

1 "That ___ a close one!"

2 Red ___ (serious warning)

3 Hard-to-please female singer

4 Important happening

5 Lion's ___ (dangerous place)

6 Person who steals wallets in broad daylight

7 To no ___ (useless)

8 Feeling stressed out

9 Large brass instrument

10 "What time ___?": 2 words

11 Person who steals from homes in the middle of the night: 2 words

18 "___ Meenie" (2010 Sean Kingston/ Justin Bieber song)

20 They might say STOP or YIELD

22 ___ up (absorb like a sponge)

24 2011 animated film about a blue macaw

27 What you eat pudding with

28 Capital of Egypt

29 "Hang in ___!"

30 Black Beauty, for one

31 Where honeybees live

32 Remove the lid from

35 Kellogg's Raisin ___

38 "I ___ your pardon?"

39 Approving word

33

ACROSS

1 "Give ___ rest!" ("Enough!"): 2 words
4 ___-control (personal sense of restraint)
8 Alternative to mousse or hairspray
11 Approve with a head gesture
12 App that lets people hire a car to take them somewhere
13 "I ___ little surprised by this": 2 words
14 Nerdy "Simpsons" character whose real name is Jeff Albertson: 3 words
17 Liquids inside printer cartridges
18 Where SpongeBob SquarePants lives
19 Red buildings on farms
21 Dirty place where pigs live
22 Computer made by Apple
25 Frosts, like a cake
26 Make a purchase
27 Trust ___ (money that parents hold for their kids)
28 Place for a pillow
29 "The lowest form of humor," supposedly
30 Examinations

31 Something to write with
32 Song that can't be sung by just one person
33 Elderly "Simpsons" character whose real name is Eleanor Abernathy: 3 words
38 Try to win something at an auction
39 Grand Theft ___ (video game series)
40 Bread that often has seeds
41 Emergency signal
42 Not far from
43 What makes a lawn moist

DOWN

1 Abbreviation at the end of many company names
2 "It's never ___ late"
3 Looked up to
4 Uses a straw
5 Flows back into the ocean
6 Feline zodiac sign
7 Snowman in a Christmas song
8 Lady ___ (pop singer)
9 Australian bird that's six feet tall
10 "Now I ___ me down to sleep"

15 Bed-and-breakfasts
16 Padlock opener
19 Food catcher around a tot's neck
20 Top card in many games
21 Source of solar energy
22 Yellow condiment, or the name of the colonel in the game Clue
23 Insect that lives in a mound
24 Round holders of music: Abbreviation
26 Paul ___ (lumberjack in folk stories)

27 "I ___ sorry for you"
29 Candy sold with collectible dispensers
30 Private teacher
31 Shoulder ___ (parts of a football uniform)
32 Facts and figures
33 "The Price Is Right" network: Abbreviation
34 ___ de Janeiro (big city in Brazil)
35 Billiards player's stick
36 It can change you into a redhead
37 Tree that sounds like "you"

ACROSS

1 Sank one's teeth into
4 Young male horse
8 Actress Watson who played Belle in the 2017 movie "Beauty and the Beast"
12 What you say when you get down to one card in a certain game
13 Two-color sandwich cookie
14 Swimming ___
15 City in southern California: 2 words
17 Teen ___ (young celebrity)
18 Family members
19 One, in a deck of cards
20 Tablet computer made by Apple
22 Very heavy metal
25 Napkin's place, often
28 Baseball player from New York
29 He slew Goliath, in the Bible
30 Winnie-___-Pooh
31 Golfer's target score
32 Hadn't yet paid
33 Catch in a net
34 "I could ___ a hand" ("Can you help me?")
36 ___ constrictor (large snake)
37 Feel the need to scratch

39 Publisher of Batman and Superman stories: 2 words
44 Sleep ___ a baby
45 "This is terrible!": 2 words
46 People in Mexico call it a siesta
47 Not as much
48 Very heavy weights
49 Pig enclosure

DOWN

1 Vehicle for schoolchildren
2 "There was an old woman who lived ___ shoe": 2 words
3 Toy vehicles that include cement mixers and bulldozers: 2 words
4 Penny, nickel, dime, or quarter
5 Metal-bearing mineral
6 Where the knee and ankle are
7 "___ much information!"
8 "Captain Underpants: The First ___ Movie"
9 Toy vehicles that run on tracks: 2 words
10 Imitate a cow
11 Once and for ___
16 "I see what you ___ there"

19 Put together, mathematically
20 Kid who's a pain in the neck
21 Small green vegetable
22 Break the ___ (do something illegal)
23 Night before a major holiday
24 First ___ kit
26 "I knew it!"
27 ___ talk (speech to a team at halftime)
29 Bambi's mother, for one
33 Actor Cruise
35 "Be nice to her! ___ your sister!"

36 Shouts from a displeased crowd
37 "Well, ___ be darned!"
38 Score that sometimes needs to be "broken"
39 On the ___ (precisely)
40 ___ Chang (girl who gave Harry Potter his first kiss)
41 Cable channel that focuses on what's happening in the world: Abbreviation
42 Animal that might use a scratching post
43 Person who might steal international secrets

ACROSS

1 Takes care of the bill
5 Garfield and Sylvester, for example
9 "The piper's son," in a nursery rhyme
12 "___, a plan, a canal—Panama!" (famous palindrome): 2 words
13 Bring into the business
14 Combat between nations
15 Website where you can find information
17 "___ not the end of the world"
18 On a ___ with (roughly equal to)
19 What happens in a story
21 ___ a finger on (touch)
24 Like toast with nothing on it
26 Fabric in fancy bedsheets
29 "It's beginning to look ___ like Christmas ...": 2 words
31 "The best is ___ to come"
33 City in western Nevada
34 Rhythm and ___ (type of music)
36 Liquid from a maple tree
38 Uncooked
39 ___ Like a Pirate Day (September 19)
41 "What you ___ is what you get"
43 Common winter virus
45 Website where you can find photos
50 Stick up, like a bank
51 Cartoon skunk ___ Le Pew
52 San Francisco's Golden ___ Bridge
53 "How much do I ___ you?" ("What's the price?")
54 Sinbad sailed seven of them
55 Have a short attention ___

DOWN

1 Monkey's hand
2 "What ___ going to do without you?": 2 words
3 Big, shaggy animal of Asia
4 A small cut made with scissors
5 Small, red fruit with a stem
6 Assistance
7 Stumble while walking
8 Closes, like an envelope
9 Website with messages limited to 280 characters
10 Grain used to make a breakfast "meal"
11 ___ Butterworth's (brand of syrup)

16 Launching ___ (rocket's platform)

20 Tool used in Olympic rowing events

21 Chemistry workplace

22 "... with liberty and justice for ___"

23 Website where you can find videos

25 "You're right"

27 ___ manner of speaking: 2 words

28 Up to ___ (so far)

30 Drink that contains caffeine

32 Has a little sip of

35 Loses one's footing

37 Split ___ soup

40 Leg joint that has a cap

42 Hens lay them

43 To and ___ (back and forth)

44 Opposite of high

46 Place where you might spend time in a steam room

47 Perform like Jay-Z

48 "Now showing ___ theater near you": 2 words

49 Adult males

36

ACROSS

1 ___ tense (verb tense for "walked" and "sang")
5 Smack with the palm of the hand
9 They sometimes appear before YouTube videos
12 Foul stench
13 Fish that's sometimes made into a casserole
14 ___ Van Winkle (book character who slept for 20 years)
15 Vehicle with a siren that might be on its way to a crime: 2 words
17 Carry ___ conversation: 2 words
18 ___-K (school for very young children)
19 State whose capital is Little Rock: Abbreviation
20 Made less wild
22 "You got that right!"
23 It's turned to start a car's ignition
24 Not common
25 Zodiac sign before Virgo
26 ___ and vigor (enthusiasm)
28 Opposite of narrow
31 Pet that purrs
32 Driver of a 15-Across

35 Changes the rough draft of an article
37 The whole shebang
38 "Do ___ say!" (parent's warning): 2 words
39 A breath of fresh ___
40 Vehicle with a siren that might be on its way to the hospital
43 Spoil, like old meat
44 Whac-A-___ (arcade game)
45 Fly on a hang glider
46 Muddy home for pigs
47 Female animals that bleat
48 That lady's

DOWN

1 ___ seed bagels
2 Be crazy about
3 Undersides of shoes
4 Prefix for "cycle" or "angular"
5 Sound system for playing music
6 Fortunate
7 Get ___ (do well at school): 2 words
8 For the most ___ (generally)

9 Inviting smell
10 Casual restaurant
11 Black card that isn't a club
16 Dessert at a wedding
21 Where a bracelet is worn
25 "Don't tell me, ___ me guess ..."
26 Amounts that things are worth
27 "___ never work!"
28 Has on, like a hat
29 Really stupid person
30 Not clean
31 What many TV watchers pay for every month
32 Boat for Pocahontas
33 Academy Award
34 Structures which some people fish from
36 "It's always the ___ old thing"
41 Trim the lawn
42 Charcoal grill waste

37

ACROSS

1 Midnight ___ (Christmas Eve event)
5 Marking on a leopard
9 ___ vera (plant that can soothe the skin)
10 Tickle Me ___ (toy based on "Sesame Street")
11 Ceramic coffee cup
14 ___ Krispies
15 Self-absorbed
16 Hindu character on "The Simpsons"
17 Hairy animal whose name also means "gab"
18 "What ___ wrong?"
19 High school dance
20 European country south of France
22 Dirty marks that detergent tries to get out
24 ___ and downs
25 In years past
26 "Little ___ has lost her sheep ...": 2 words
29 Bad signs of the future
31 Icons on an iPad screen
32 Garment often worn after a soak in the tub
34 Assistant to Santa

36 Insect that could be a queen or a drone
37 Exist
38 "When You Wish Upon a ___" (song from "Pinocchio")
39 Army ___ (kind of insect)
40 Unbeatable cards in some games
41 Sergeant Snorkel's dog in "Beetle Bailey"
42 It helps pass down traits from your parents
43 "Things aren't as bad as they ___"

DOWN

1 "Quite contrary" girl in a nursery rhyme
2 Criminal's fake name
3 You put it over your hand and make it talk: 2 words
4 "I can't ___ why not!"
5 Half of fourteen
6 Prepare for the future
7 Leaves out
8 2,000 pounds

11 You move it with strings and make it talk

12 "Once ___ a time ..."

13 Pink tissues around the teeth

18 Intelligent

19 It gets turned in a book

21 Animals like King Kong

23 Gentle, like a house pet

26 Ali ___ (hero who found a magic lamp)

27 "Yes, we're ___" (sign in a store window)

28 How much something costs

29 Very, very fat

30 Mr. ___ (Fred Flintstone's boss)

33 You cook things in it

35 Go ___ bad to worse

37 Trail behind

38 Signal from a sinking ship

ACROSS

1 Steal from
4 Fruit that's often found in fruit cocktail
8 "The ___ Bitsy Spider"
12 One of Dumbo's "wings"
13 Live a life of ___ (have few problems)
14 ___-false test
15 Athlete in the major leagues
16 Small household containers for garbage: 2 words
18 "We'll cross that bridge ___ we come to it"
20 Reaction to an amazing magic trick
21 Someone who possesses something
23 What Picasso and Rembrandt created
24 Long part of a crocodile's head
27 Wild animal's home
28 Explosive that's used for demolition: Abbreviation
29 The Kentucky Derby, for one
30 Cover up gray hair
31 Place a wager
32 Walked back and forth nervously
33 Bring a court case against

34 Building that hires tellers
35 Large industrial containers for garbage
39 Declare
42 Where India and Pakistan are
43 Warmth
44 "I believe you ___ me an explanation"
45 Greatest
46 "You better get back here, or ___!"
47 What's attached to a basketball hoop

DOWN

1 Democrat's opponent: Abbreviation
2 Rower's tool
3 Chocolatey dessert that sometimes contains nuts
4 ___ Cottontail
5 Deserve
6 Proud ___ peacock: 2 words
7 Health ___ (spa)
8 Back scratcher's target
9 ___-la-la (song sounds)
10 Light source for Earth
11 Word of agreement
17 ___ Wheels (brand of toy cars)

19 Not him
21 "___ MacDonald Had a Farm"
22 Out of harm's ___ (safe)
23 Insect that's attracted to spilled food
24 "Thriller" singer Michael
25 ___ of spades (highest-ranking card in bridge)
26 Get married to
28 What babies do when their molars first start coming in
29 Scampered away

31 School transportation
32 Sticky stuff that's used when you make a collage
33 Small argument
34 Undergarments with cups and straps
35 Pat lightly with a napkin
36 Do something with
37 Prefix for "pronounce" or "understanding"
38 Fish that looks like a snake
40 "I'm in ___ of your achievement"
41 Until now

39

ACROSS

1 Game show host Sajak
4 Animals that supply milk
8 Not warm, but not freezing
12 Mineral resource in the video game Minecraft
13 Make changes to a manuscript
14 The point ___ return: 2 words
15 When an assignment is due
17 "___ first you don't succeed, try, try again": 2 words
18 Ginger ___ (soda from Canada Dry)
19 What Humpty Dumpty sat on
21 Mr. ___ (animal with a "Wild Ride" at Disneyland)
24 Lend a hand to
25 "This ___ job for Superman!": 2 words
28 "___ Baba and the Forty Thieves"
29 Looked directly at
31 Homer's neighbor on "The Simpsons" who says "Okely-dokely!"
32 Pay-___-view movie
33 Insect that can live in a farm or a hill
34 Acquires

35 Belly button fuzz
37 Dessert with a flaky crust
39 Abrasive stuff on sandpaper
41 Phrase at the top of a newspaper article
46 Section of a window
47 Sinister
48 Period of 24 hours
49 Thin part of a dandelion
50 ___ mortals (regular people)
51 That girl

DOWN

1 Like two peas in a ___
2 "What ___ you waiting for?"
3 Hot drink that's popular in China
4 Mobile phone
5 Garfield's canine companion
6 Beat the other team
7 Baby on "Family Guy"
8 Shape of a Slinky
9 Not on the computer
10 Like a bump ___ log: 2 words
11 Whole bunch
16 Father, to his kids
20 Do simple math
21 Woodpecker's sound

Crossword grid with numbered cells: 1, 2, 3, 4, 5, 6, 7, 8, 9, 10, 11, 12, 13, 14, 15, 16, 17, 18, 19, 20, 21, 22, 23, 24, 25, 26, 27, 28, 29, 30, 31, 32, 33, 34, 35, 36, 37, 38, 39, 40, 41, 42, 43, 44, 45, 46, 47, 48, 49, 50, 51

22 What to yell when the matador avoids the bull

23 Delta or United, for example

24 Perform a role in a movie

26 "I had my heart ___ on it"

27 What many pages in fashion magazines are

29 Appliance that's mostly used during hot weather

30 Nation's official song, like "The Star-Spangled Banner"

34 Substance for styling hair

36 Collector's ___ (rare object)

37 Two of a kind

38 Doing nothing

39 Device that provides driving directions: Abbreviation

40 Ron Weasley's pet Scabbers, for one

42 She was tempted by a serpent

43 Age verification cards: Abbreviation

44 Opposite of "yeah"

45 Keep an ___ on (watch closely)

ACROSS

1 "This ___ nothing to do with you"

4 Break-___ (illegal entries)

7 It holds a purse over your shoulder

12 Ending for "patriot" or "hero"

13 It's used to fire arrows

14 Wooden shipping box

15 Language that's spoken in Beijing

17 Become juicy and ready to eat

18 Carry with difficulty

19 ___ Levine (lead singer of Maroon 5)

21 Limerick, for example

23 What a red light means

24 ___ mode (like some desserts): 2 words

27 Language that's spoken in Cairo

29 Language that's spoken in Berlin

31 Moist

32 Mechanics' oily cloths

34 As ___ as pie

35 Drifter who rode on freight trains, once

36 Candy that comes in small rectangular "bricks"

37 Material used in some gloves and neckties

40 Language that's spoken in Rome

44 ___ Oyl (Popeye's girlfriend)

45 Silent "yes"

46 League for very tall athletes: Abbreviation

47 Ran a towel over

48 Fuel for a car

49 "Family ___" (animated comedy)

DOWN

1 Hawaiian Punch competitor: Hyphenated

2 Charcoal grill waste

3 Give a grin to: 2 words

4 "___ to differ!": 2 words

5 Rejections

6 Perspire

7 Minor injury to the skin

8 Quick haircut

9 Music genre for Drake

10 Dined

11 Ballpoint or quill

16 Lacking feeling

20 Raining cats and ___

21 Rabbit's foot

22 Stuff that's picked out of a mine

23 It forms over a healing wound

24 "The ___ Race" (reality show where teams travel around the world)

25 ___ Vegas, Nevada

26 By ___ means necessary

28 Smoothed the wrinkles out of

30 Rod and ___ (fishing gear)

33 Coming and ___

35 Where bees make honey

36 Knee ___ (protection for some athletes)

37 Piglet's mother

38 Three-time heavyweight boxing champion Muhammad

39 Helpful hint

41 Come ___ screeching halt: 2 words

42 Aladdin's pet monkey, in the movie

43 How people in the Congress vote "no"

ANSWERS

1

S	T	O	P		B	U	D		L	I	F	T
P	A	U	L		U	S	E		I	D	E	A
A	C	R	O	S	S	A	N	D	D	O	W	N
			W	E	T		N	O	S			
R	I	V	E	T		B	I	G		C	A	T
A	C	I	D		B	U	S		F	A	T	E
G	Y	M		I	A	M		J	A	P	A	N
			A	N	N		E	A	T			
B	L	A	C	K	A	N	D	W	H	I	T	E
A	I	N	T		N	A	G		E	V	I	L
N	E	T	S		A	P	E		R	E	E	K

2

B	E	A	D		T	W	O		P	A	N
R	E	L	I	C		H	A	M		O	W	E
A	L	L	A	H		E	Y	E		S	E	W
			L	I	S	A		N	O	T		
P	T	A		L	A	V	A		F	A	L	L
J	U	S	T	I	C	E	L	E	A	G	U	E
S	T	U	N		K	N	O	X		E	G	G
		S	T	Y		G	E	T	S			
Y	O	U		E	W	E		R	O	B	O	T
A	L	A		T	A	R		A	L	O	N	E
M	E	L		I	D	S		O	X	E	N

3

S	A	W		H	O	P	E		S	P	A	R
O	N	E		A	R	E	A		K	A	T	E
S	T	E	E	L	E	R	S		I	C	E	D
			Y	O	O		T	A	S	K		
H	A	V	E		B	E	G		E	B	B
A	L	I		T	H	E	R	E		R	O	O
Y	A	K		W	A	D		I	S	P	Y
		I	R	O	N		G	A	S			
N	I	N	A		S	E	A	H	A	W	K	S
E	D	G	Y		E	G	G	O		H	I	P
T	O	S	S		L	O	S	T		O	N	A

4

C	O	P	S		S	H	E		H	A	T
A	U	R	A		N	A	B		O	B	I
B	R	O	N	T	O	S	A	U	R	U	S
			D	U	O		Y	R	S		
B	A	G		G	P	S		L	E	M	O	N
A	R	A	B		Y	E	S		S	A	N	E
A	T	B	A	T		A	P	P		D	E	W
			L	O	S		I	T	S			
V	E	L	O	C	I	R	A	P	T	O	R
A	Y	E		A	S	A		I	O	W	A
N	E	T		N	H	L		T	E	N	T

5

B	O	B		T	E	A		R	A	B	I	D
I	N	A		O	A	R		A	B	O	V	E
G	E	T	L	O	S	T		P	L	A	Y	S
		H	I	N	T		P	I	E	R		
R	U	I	N	S		B	A	D		D	A	B
I	S	N	T		B	U	Y		I	S	L	E
B	E	G		O	U	T		A	C	H	E	D
		S	I	P	S		O	R	E	O		
C	A	U	S	E		G	U	M	D	R	O	P
A	L	I	E	N		A	C	E		T	R	I
B	I	T	E	S		P	H	D		S	E	T

6

B	E	A	R		A	D	E		A	C	T	S
E	G	G	O		D	O	C		I	O	W	A
G	O	O	D	N	I	G	H	T	M	O	O	N
			S	A	D		O	U	I			
P	A	R		G	A	S		G	N	A	T	S
O	H	I	O		S	A	T		G	L	E	E
T	A	M	P	A		M	A	D		L	E	T
			E	S	P		S	O	N			
H	A	R	R	I	E	T	T	H	E	S	P	Y
A	R	E	A		T	O	E		W	I	R	E
W	E	D	S		S	O	D		S	P	O	T

7

S	O	D	A	S		T	I	M		J	O	B
A	R	E	N	A		I	D	O		E	W	E
P	A	T	T	Y		S	E	A	T	T	L	E
		R	I	N	G		A	N	O			
B	R	O		O	A	K		A	S	H	E	S
R	A	I	D		S	I	R		S	O	S	O
A	T	T	I	C		T	I	C		U	P	S
			S	E	E		D	O	C	S		
C	H	I	C	A	G	O		M	O	T	T	O
R	O	N		S	O	N		A	L	O	H	A
Y	E	N		E	S	E		S	A	N	E	R

8

H	A	S		C	B	S		S	T	I	R
A	B	U		L	I	T		I	V	O	R	Y
M	E	N		A	T	A		S	E	N	S	E
	D	A	Y		I	S	A	N				
A	T	O	M		O	R	C	A		P	U	P
R	O	W	I	N	G	M	A	C	H	I	N	E
K	E	N		I	R	A	N		I	G	O	R
		A	G	E	S		A	P	E			
P	I	T	C	H		T	I	N		O	D	D
E	V	E	N	T		E	N	D		N	O	R
G	E	N	E			R	A	Y		S	T	Y

9

C	U	P		A	C	T	S		B	R	A	N
A	S	A		B	L	U	E		R	A	G	E
M	U	S	I	C	A	L	C	H	A	I	R	S
E	A	T	S		W	I	R	E		N	E	T
	L	A	L	A		P	E	R		Y	E	S
			E	B	B		T	E	N			
L	E	G		O	R	A		S	O	C	K	
A	P	R		V	A	N	S		A	L	A	S
S	C	A	V	E	N	G	E	R	H	U	N	T
T	O	T	O		D	E	M	I		E	G	O
S	T	E	W		S	L	I	P		S	A	W

10

J	A	R	S		V	A	T		A	F	E	W
U	T	A	H		A	L	E		B	I	T	E
G	A	T	E		C	A	L		O	N	C	E
		A	S	I	A		L	O	U	D		
C	O	T		D	N	A		S	T	I	L	T
B	O	O		A	T	T	I	C		N	O	R
S	H	U	S	H		O	R	A		G	U	Y
			I	P	O	D		I	R	O	N	
P	A	L	E		A	B	S		V	E	T	O
A	X	L	E		T	I	E		A	M	E	N
W	E	E	D		A	D	S		L	O	N	E

11

P	A	S	S		C	A	R	S		B	U	S
E	X	I	T		R	I	O	T		A	S	K
W	E	R	E		A	R	B	O	R	D	A	Y
			M	T	V		E	W	E			
C	O	P		R	E	P		D	A	R	E	
P	R	E	S	I	D	E	N	T	S	D	A	Y
R	A	G	U		N	O	W		D	Y	E	
			M	O	O		T	O	M			
L	A	B	O	R	D	A	Y		A	P	E	S
I	C	E		A	I	R	E		S	A	V	E
P	E	T		L	E	F	T		S	T	E	W

12

C	O	B		A	M	A		S	H	O	W
O	W	E		C	A	B		P	I	A	N	O
P	L	A	S	T	I	C		A	L	I	E	N
	U	P	O	N		O	D	O	R			
A	L	T	A	R		B	U	S		D	R	Y
B	A	Y	S		H	U	T		T	R	U	E
U	P	S		E	A	T		P	O	E	T	S
			A	W	A	Y		H	I	T	S	
F	I	L	E	S		G	E	N	E	S	I	S
I	V	O	R	Y		A	R	T		E	G	O
G	E	N	E			L	E	O		R	O	W

13

M	U	S	T		M	A	S	H		J	I	M
A	S	I	A		A	R	E	A		A	C	E
C	A	R	P	E	N	T	E	R		N	E	T
			E	A	T		S	E	M	I		
J	O	B		R	I	B		S	A	T	I	N
A	R	U	G		S	A	W		D	O	V	E
W	A	T	E	R		D	A	D		R	E	D
		C	L	O	T		S	O	S			
B	A	H		A	R	C	H	I	T	E	C	T
A	G	E		D	U	N	E		E	V	A	N
N	O	R		S	E	N	D		W	E	N	T

14

A	S	A		P	T	A		P	I	T	A
G	U	N		R	A	N		A	D	A	M
O	B	I	W	A	N	K	E	N	O	B	I
			M	A	Y		L	E	E		
L	O	R	A	X		G	E	L		J	O	Y
O	R	A	L		P	U	T		B	O	N	E
G	E	M		P	A	Y		P	A	G	E	S
			A	I	R		F	A	N			
P	A	D	M	E	A	M	I	D	A	L	A
A	L	O	E		D	E	N		N	E	T
T	E	E	N		E	N	D		A	X	E

15

C	A	U	S	E		P	A	C		B	O	W
A	P	R	O	N		E	G	O		U	F	O
B	U	L	L	D	O	Z	E	R		L	A	W
			D	E	N		S	E	L	L		
L	A	B		D	E	W		S	I	D	E	S
A	T	U	B		S	O	W		D	O	V	E
P	A	L	E	R		N	O	T		G	E	T
		L	E	O	S		O	I	L			
P	U	P		B	U	L	L	F	I	G	H	T
U	S	E		O	R	E		F	L	O	U	R
T	A	N		T	E	E		S	O	O	T	Y

16

B	A	D		C	D	S		P	I	L	O	T
U	S	E		R	A	W		A	R	E	N	A
T	A	N		A	M	I		T	A	T	E	R
		M	A	N		T	H	I	N			
S	H	A	D	E		Z	O	O		B	O	W
E	A	R	S		J	E	T		L	E	I	A
A	S	K		C	A	R		W	E	L	L	S
			H	O	W	L		H	O	G		
S	A	T	I	N		A	T	E		I	S	H
A	L	I	V	E		N	O	R		U	N	O
W	I	P	E	S		D	Y	E		M	O	W

17

A	S	H		R	O	L	L		O	D	D	S
T	E	A		O	R	E	O		P	R	O	P
M	E	R	M	A	I	D	S		E	A	S	Y
			R	I	D		I	N	C			
P	A	Y	S		W	A	T	T		O	W	N
A	P	P		T	A	X	E	S		M	O	O
L	E	O		E	D	E	N		J	A	W	S
			T	H	E		O	I	L			
S	I	T	E		G	I	R	A	F	F	E	S
O	V	E	R		U	S	E	R		O	W	E
N	E	R	D		M	A	P	S		Y	E	T

18

P	A	T	H		C	A	L	L		N	A	P
A	C	R	E		A	R	E	A		O	N	E
N	E	I	L	A	R	M	S	T	R	O	N	G
			P	I	T		S	E	E	D		
P	A	W		M	E	T		R	A	L	P	H
A	B	A	D		R	O	O		L	E	I	A
D	E	L	I	S		P	R	O		S	E	T
			T	A	P	S		P	U	G		
B	U	Z	Z	L	I	G	H	T	Y	E	A	R
U	S	E		I	D	E	A		M	A	R	E
G	A	S		T	E	E	N		S	T	E	P

19

```
MATCH GET  KEY
ALOHA ALE  IMA
CLEAR LINEDUP
   TELL  TAN
HRS SOBS  SEAT
BOTH ALI  TYPE
OBOE DAZE  SEE
  MRS  DEAD
SLASHED  ROMAN
PAC IVE  TRACE
ASH PER  HATED
```

20

```
ACTS DAY  RAT
SOAP ALE  AGE
ABBREVIATION
   SAX  HEN
ATA TIPS  ABEL
DOTS TOT  MOVE
SOLE SEAM  WET
 AND  RAW
CONTRACTIONS
ANT ERA  NOAH
TEA WEB  EDGE
```

21

```
CAMP THAW  TAR
AREA RACE  IDO
BILLGATES  GOD
LET IVE  THERE
ESS REDS  OREO
  ALL  LEG
FAWN SEED  ART
ALONE VEG  HOE
DIM STEVEJOBS
EVE PINE  ALOT
DEN NETS  WETS
```

22

```
TAME MAP  ASKS
ASIA EGO  POET
PAST EEL  PUNY
  SEAT  LAST
FAIRS HEN  HAT
ITS THING  DIE
GAS RIP  LLAMA
  IPOD SEEK
RIPE DOT  MOAT
IMPS EWE  OTTO
BAIT NEW  NAME
```

23

```
UTAH STIR  TAN
POSE TACO  UGH
STARBUCKS  GEL
  BED  SOB
ADS LIAR  NOPE
LITTLECAESARS
IDEA SEND  TOP
  AXE  SEW
RAM MCDONALDS
OWE MAIM  YOYO
WED APES  STEW
```

24

```
APPS BIB  ACTS
CLUE ARE  SHIN
EAST BAG  HERO
SIS PANIC  SEW
 NICER  NOAHS
 NON  ALI
 TBONE  STARS
TWO YANKS  EAR
RIOT TOA  ACNE
INTO EST  BATS
PEST RYE  STAT
```

25

```
TAP  MALL   POTS
ISA  OREO   AREA
CINNAMON   WENT
      ONS  GANG
TOPS   GET   ACE
INA  WHERE   NOW
PER  EEL    GONE
  SODA   ANY
BALD  ROSEMARY
AGED   TRIO   CUE
TOYS   SEAN   TNT
```

26

```
      TIED   SHAG
STU  ACRE   LIFE
PUN  MEAN   OGRE
UNITE   SIS   HES
RAVE   EEK   SEE
  ENDS   DISC
GRR  ALL    UHOH
HAS  DIE   SNORE
ODIE   CAGE   ONE
SITS   EVEN   LOL
TOYS   SEED
```

27

```
HATS   ASK   THY
ACHOO   GIN   WEE
STILL  ELEMENT
  READ   KEEN
TOT  FUR   SATAN
WAYS   DOH   TYPE
OFFER   BIB   FEW
  IGOR   JEDI
CARAMEL  SOFAS
UPS  ABE   TITLE
BUT  NAG    THAW
```

28

```
ASH  ADAM   HUFF
PEA  CONE   ASIA
PAN  HANDSTAND
  DOE    DIE
IDOL  BALD   HAT
LOUD   EYE   PAIR
LOT  ICES   ANDY
  ONA    ADD
HANDCUFFS   BAN
IPOD   SEEK   AGE
PEWS   EWES   GOT
```

29

```
ACHE   DAWN
SHOE   ERIE   OWE
KICK   SENT   PEA
EMU  PEN   SCENT
DES  ARTS   ANTS
  PINT   TAPS
IRON   SEEN   EGG
ROCKS   LED   SIR
IOU  LAMP   LAVA
STS  ABEL   AMEN
  PURE   BEND
```

30

```
TED  LOW   SATIN
ICE  OWE   ABONE
LONDONENGLAND
  TOPS   AGE
SPINS   SPY   COP
EAST   DOS   COLA
ANT  FOX   CANDY
  SAW   HALT
BERLINGERMANY
AWAIT   ARE   COO
TENTH   GOD   TWO
```

31

```
SOS   PUT   CUTE
ANY   AHA   CANOE
GEM   SUGARBOWL
  BATH   DOS
ADORE   PAW   COT
TILE   MOM   HALO
ADS   BAD   HANDY
   SAN   FIND
COOKIEJAR   LAB
ORBIT   ACE   EYE
WAIT   YES   SEE
```

32

```
   WADED   PAT
TIC   ALIVE   IVE
USA   SEVEN   CAN
BITE   RAN   SKIS
ATBEST   TRIPLE
   UNO   IGO
SCRIPT   HONCHO
PAGE   HBO   SKIP
OIL   BERRY   EVE
ORA   ERASE   TEN
NOR   GENES
```

33

```
ITA   SELF   GEL
NOD   UBER   AMA
COMICBOOKGUY
   INKS   SEA
BARNS   STY   MAC
ICES   BUY   FUND
BED   PUN   TESTS
   PEN   DUET
CRAZYCATLADY
BID   AUTO   RYE
SOS   NEAR   DEW
```

34

```
BIT   COLT   EMMA
UNO   OREO   POOL
SANDIEGO   IDOL
   KIN   ACE
IPAD   LEAD   LAP
MET   DAVID   THE
PAR   OWED   TRAP
   USE   BOA
ITCH   DCCOMICS
LIKE   OHNO   NAP
LESS   TONS   STY
```

35

```
PAYS   CATS   TOM
AMAN   HIRE   WAR
WIKIPEDIA   ITS
   PAR   PLOT
LAY   DRY   SATIN
ALOT   YET   RENO
BLUES   SAP   RAW
   TALK   SEE
FLU   INSTAGRAM
ROB   PEPE   GATE
OWE   SEAS   SPAN
```

36

```
PAST   SLAP   ADS
ODOR   TUNA   RIP
POLICECAR   ONA
PRE   ARK   TAMED
YES   KEY   RARE
   LEO   VIM
WIDE   CAT   COP
EDITS   ALL   ASI
AIR   AMBULANCE
ROT   MOLE   SOAR
STY   EWES   HERS
```

37

```
M A S S   S P O T
A L O E   E L M O   M U G
R I C E   V A I N   A P U
Y A K   W E N T   P R O M
  S P A I N   S T A I N S
    U P S     A G O
B O P E E P   O M E N S
A P P S   R O B E   E L F
B E E   L I V E   S T A R
A N T   A C E S   O T T O
      G E N E   S E E M
```

38

```
R O B   P E A R   I T S Y
E A R   E A S E   T R U E
P R O   T R A S H C A N S
    W H E N   O O H
O W N E R   A R T   J A W
L A I R   T N T   R A C E
D Y E   B E T   P A C E D
    S U E   B A N K
D U M P S T E R S   S A Y
A S I A   H E A T   O W E
B E S T   E L S E   N E T
```

39

```
P A T   C O W S   C O O L
O R E   E D I T   O F N O
D E A D L I N E   I F A T
    A L E   W A L L
T O A D   A I D   I S A
A L I   F A C E D   N E D
P E R   A N T   G E T S
    L I N T   P I E
G R I T   H E A D L I N E
P A N E   E V I L   D A Y
S T E M   M E R E   S H E
```

40

```
H A S   I N S   S T R A P
I S M   B O W   C R A T E
C H I N E S E   R I P E N
    L U G   A D A M
P O E M   S T O P   A L A
A R A B I C   G E R M A N
W E T   R A G S   E A S Y
    H O B O   P E Z
S A T I N   I T A L I A N
O L I V E   N O D   N B A
W I P E D   G A S   G U Y
```

ALSO AVAILABLE

ABOUT THE AUTHOR

TRIP PAYNE is a professional puzzle constructor and editor from Sherman Oaks, California. He made his first puzzles when he was in elementary school, had his first puzzle in a national magazine when he was in high school, and worked for a major puzzle magazine when he was in college. He has made kids' puzzles for such places as *Scholastic News*, *Games Junior*, and *TV Guide*. You can visit his website at tripleplaypuzzles.com and follow him on Twitter @PuzzleTrip.

PUZZLE
WRIGHT
JUNIOR

JUNIOR New York

An Imprint of Sterling Publishing Co., Inc.
1166 Avenue of the Americas
New York, NY 10036

ISBN 978-1-4549-3155-3

Distributed in Canada by Sterling Publishing Co., Inc.
c/o Canadian Manda Group, 664 Annette Street
Toronto, Ontario M6S 2C8, Canada
Distributed in the United Kingdom by GMC Distribution Services
Castle Place, 166 High Street, Lewes, East Sussex BN7 1XU, England
Distributed in Australia by NewSouth Books,
University of New South Wales, Sydney, NSW 2052, Australia

For information about custom editions, special sales, and premium and
corporate purchases, please contact Sterling Special Sales at 800-805-5489
or specialsales@sterlingpublishing.com.

Manufactured in Canada
Lot #:
2 4 6 8 10 9 7 5 3 1
11/18

sterlingpublishing.com
puzzlewright.com

CROSSWORD PUZZLES

for the WEEKEND!

TRIP PAYNE

JUNIOR